TALK

TALK

MICHAEL NATHANSON

PLAYWRIGHTS CANADA PRESS

Talk © Copyright 2009 Michael Nathanson

PLAYWRIGHTS CANADA PRESS
The Canadian Drama Publisher
215 Spadina Ave., Suite 230, Toronto, Ontario, Canada, M5T 2C7
phone 416.703.0013   fax 416.408.3402
orders@playwrightscanada.com • www.playwrightscanada.com

The publisher acknowledges the support of the Canadian taxpayers through the
Government of Canada Book Publishing Industry Development Program, the
Canada Council for the Arts, the Ontario Arts Council, and the Ontario Media
Development Corporation.

Cover and type design by Blake Sproule
Photography by Steve Salnikowski
Interior photos depict Michael Rubenfeld as Josh
and Matthew TenBruggencate as Gordon

LIBRARY AND ARCHIVES CANADA CATALOGUING IN PUBLICATION

Nathanson, Michael, 1966-
Talk / Michael Nathanson.

A play.
ISBN 978-0-88754-873-4

I. Title.

PS8627.A794T35 2009   C812'.6   C2009-900107-1

First edition: January 2009
Printed and bound by Canadian Printco, Scarborough, Ontario, Canada

FOR REBECCA, WITH LOVE, ALWAYS

On September 11, 2001, my wife and I were living in New York City. We were supposed to have been downtown around 8:45 a.m. Our plans were to have our civil wedding ceremony that morning with a friend witnessing for us and then the three of us would spend the rest of the day celebrating. To get downtown from our far-north position in Manhattan required the famous A Train of song. Our stop on the A Train line for that morning would have been the Chambers Street stop, otherwise known as the World Trade Center stop. Due to a weird feeling the day before, I did not confirm our plans with our witness-to-be and none of us headed downtown.

About a month after this event, having fled New York City to regroup in the serenity of Palm Springs, California, I received an email from a dear friend who was living overseas. The email contained writings from the political left, much of them centred on the recent terrorist attack. One email in particular caught my attention. It was written by an American professor and it was a rant against the evils committed by the Jews towards the Palestinians. As the character Josh says in the play (and as Billy Crystal once said in character as Buddy Young Jr.), "Folks, I'm a Jew." I did not understand how a friend, someone I considered to be a very close friend, could send me such an email at any time, but especially so given the context of recent events.

That email was the impetus for *Talk*. The play, despite its origins, is not autobiographical. I wanted to write a play that ultimately dealt with the dissolution of friendship. How do we get to that point where things fall apart? And the timeless question: How well do we really know anyone? The political arguments contained within the play are important to the characters, but they exist both as reasoned thinking and shameless hyperbole. My great hope for the play is that it would engender dialogue around both subjects, and it was my true privilege to have watched it do so in production. I hope reading the script gives you plenty to talk about as well.

Talk received its world premiere at Winnipeg Jewish Theatre (WJT), Winnipeg, Manitoba, in October 2007. It was performed at the Berney Theatre with the following cast:

JOSH   Michael Rubenfeld
GORDON   Matthew TenBruggencate

Director: Ross McMillan
Set & Costume Design: Abigail Myers
Lighting Design: Randy Harder
Stage Manager: Sylvia Fisher
Dramaturge: Per Brask

In normal type, the characters speak in direct address. In quotation marks, they speak to each other.

The actors are seated.

JOSH   The question is simple.

GORDON   "So what do you think of her?"

JOSH   "What do I think of her?"

GORDON   "Yeah. What do you think of her?" It's a simple question.

JOSH   A very simple question.

     "I've only just met her."

GORDON   "Well, I know that."

JOSH   "I mean, I'm sure she was nervous."

GORDON   "I'm sure she was."

     I'm sure she was.

JOSH   I had to say something. I mean, this woman was being offered to me—offered to me, that sounds terrible—she was being offered up to me, shown to me, I knew what she meant to Gordon—

GORDON   He knew what she meant to me.

JOSH   It was obvious. The way he spoke of her. Over the phone? Are you kidding me? The emails I got? What more could you want for your friend? The happiness dripped off each word he spoke, each sentence written. Finally, I thought. After the divorce, which was a train wreck—don't ask—through with the depression, he did what we all do and what we all think is impossible: He stumbled into it.

GORDON   I wasn't expecting Clotilde. I had given up hope, was past hope, and then one night, at a friend's place for dinner—

JOSH   He meets her one night at friend's, a potluck dinner, the day after, he called me—

GORDON   I had called up Josh.

JOSH   He said to me:

GORDON   "I don't think it's going to happen for me."

JOSH   "You're fulla' shit."

GORDON   "I mean, and it's okay, I've come to accept it, but some people just— "

JOSH   "Gordon, that's defeatist. Just remember this."

GORDON   "What?"

JOSH   "One: You're an incredible person."

GORDON   "Okay."

JOSH	"And two: You never know. Okay? You never know."
GORDON	And you don't. And then I met Clotilde.
JOSH	The stories he told me. How much love he felt. The beauty of the world. The icky stuff that we all love to hear, he was saying it.
GORDON	I always hoped for—no, that's too weak—I had always dreamed, I guess, believed, quietly, that in the back of my heart, this notion, this love I believed in—
JOSH	And what do you do when you're in love? You want to share it with the world. You want the whole world to see your happiness, revel in your happiness. Nothing more could I want for my friend. Nothing more.
GORDON	Because, and you see, this is important for me. Not to, you understand, not to get their approval, my friend's approval, because, because my relationship with Clotilde is between me and her and no one else—but, you know, I do want him to like her. So we arrange to meet Josh. And we do. And it goes well.
JOSH	The lounge at Rae and Jerry's. How could it not go well?
GORDON	And Clotilde, being the person she is, she gives us boys some alone time, so we can talk. Because she understands what this friendship means to me. And living overseas, we get so little time together.
JOSH	I don't see Gordon that often. He's in London now. The good one, not the Ontario one. Fucking Brit, 'e is now. But it's good to see him. Jesus, it's good to see him. Twelve years now, this one. That's a long time.

GORDON   Because I trust him like few others. His opinion. Not that— (*pause*) I mean, why wouldn't he like her?

JOSH   And why wouldn't I like her? She's bright, she's funny, she's attractive, she's—okay, I looked—she's got a great body, and ABOVE ALL, she absolutely loves my friend. She loves Gordon. What else is there?

GORDON   "I'm sure she was."

JOSH   "Hey, I was nervous."

GORDON   "You? Why?"

JOSH   "'Cause Gord, I know what she means to you. I don't want to put my foot in my mouth, give her a bad impression of your past or anything."

GORDON   "I'm my past. I mean, Josh, me. I'm my past. So if she's going to get a bad impression—"

JOSH   "No, you're right, you're right. I don't know. I was nervous, what can I tell you?"

GORDON   "Well, so was she."

JOSH   "So there you go. How 'bout you?"

GORDON   "Yeah. Me too."

JOSH   "Three for three, a perfect day."

GORDON   "A perfect day."

JOSH   "A triple and we woulda hit for the cycle."

GORDON   And he still hasn't answered the question.

JOSH   Once in a while you're either lucky enough or
           unlucky enough, depending on your disposition, you
           see future trouble looming right in front of you. It's
           the golem in the middle of the room but only you
           have the ability to see it. And you have a choice. You
           can choose not to mention it and everyone can go on
           with his or her own business. Or you can tell them
           there's a golem in the room and just hope no one gets
           trampled too badly.

GORDON   Because when you ask someone a question and they
           don't answer you… it's rude. And you think friends
           would be beyond. Such behaviour.

JOSH   So he asks me again.

GORDON   "So what'd you think of her?"

JOSH   "Well, I told you."

GORDON   "You told me she was nervous."

JOSH   "Wasn't she?"

GORDON   "I told you yes. Then you said you were nervous."

JOSH   "I was."

GORDON   "But that still doesn't give me your impression of her."

JOSH   "Hey, I don't do impressions."

GORDON   "You're hilarious."

JOSH   "Fifty million Chinese can't be wrong."

GORDON   "Joshie—"

JOSH   "Gordon—"

GORDON   "What did you think of Clotilde?"

JOSH   And I don't know what to tell him.

GORDON   And he pauses again.

JOSH   I know the longer I take the worse it gets. Because, as humans, in the absence of information, we will rush to fill that void with any story that makes sense to us. With complete disregard for what the truth may be.

GORDON   The longer he takes the more I worry. Because I love Clotilde. I love her so much and he should be happy for me. He knows how badly I've wanted this. Is he jealous? But he shouldn't be. Maybe he is. Maybe he's attracted to Clotilde because... because she's very beautiful and he can be very arrogant at times. I love Josh, but it's true. He can be arrogant. I wish I could ask Clotilde right now. She would know. She can tell these things. If he was attracted, if his eyes drifted.

JOSH   She is attractive. I'm not jealous. I mean, good for him. I'm sure it is. But, and I know he's thinking this, he's thinking it's a man/woman thing and it's not.

GORDON   So maybe, maybe this silence is suggestive, maybe this silence is instructing me that the three of us can't be together as friends. Maybe, maybe Josh's trying to make me choose, maybe he thinks—

JOSH   "I like her."

GORDON   "It took you a long time to say it."

JOSH   "I like her. I felt nervous."

GORDON   "Then why couldn't you just say, 'I like her.'"

JOSH   "I just did."

GORDON   "I had to ask you twice."

JOSH   "I like to play hard to get."

GORDON   "I've never known you to shut up."

JOSH   "First time for everything."

GORDON   "Josh, I can't believe you're telling me the truth."

JOSH   "I am telling you the truth."

GORDON   "I don't believe you."

JOSH   "On my grandmother's grave."

GORDON   "I don't believe you."

JOSH   "On the Torah."

GORDON   "I still don't believe you."

JOSH   "Gordon, if you don't believe me, how'm I gonna convince you?"

GORDON   "I'll know."

JOSH   "You'll know?"

GORDON   "Yes. I'll be able to tell."

JOSH   "Gordon, I like her."

I did like her. Bright, conversant, charming. That's what she is. She knows who I am to Gordon and wanted to make an impression. Wanted to belong. Biggest compliment of any girlfriend or boyfriend that ever came down the pike for any of my friends: They could hang. You know? You meet someone's partner for the first time and it's easy like a Sunday morning. There was the occasional conversational lapse, however—

GORDON   —she's French—

JOSH   —she's French—but she can hang.

"I like her."

GORDON   "For real?"

JOSH   "I like her. What higher compliment can I give?"

GORDON   "Okay. *(pause)* I believe you."

JOSH   "Well thank God for that."

GORDON   I don't believe him. I don't believe Josh. Because if he had just said it, if he had spontaneously responded, fine then. Okay. I'll accept that. But to pause?

JOSH   I shouldn't have paused.

GORDON   To have paused twice?

JOSH   I should have just said something. 'She's great.' 'Nice rack.'
              I kid. But each time he asked—

GORDON   Because I'm going to marry this woman. I can feel it. It's a
              feeling you get. And you know. And I've seen no one but
              Josh as my best man. Make everything right the second
              time. And I can. Because I know.

JOSH   Each time he asked, I saw that goddamned golem. I saw
              that enormous beast just ready to tip its weight over onto
              the two of us and I couldn't quite see an exit strategy.
              I thought about the Dalai Lama—truly—and taking a
              higher road because our friendship is more important
              than anything. Than any words misspoke. Than any—

              "I love you, Gordon."

GORDON   "Well I love you, Josh."

JOSH   "And I'm sorry, about—I'm getting weird here."

GORDON   "I can see that."

JOSH   "And it's stupid. Stupid of me. I don't know what I'm
              doing."

GORDON   "Listen, if you have a problem with Clotilde, if there's
              something you didn't like, that's fine. You're my friend. I
              love you and respect you. And I'd be curious to get your
              opinion of her. That's all. Not that it matters, because I
              love Clotilde regardless. Regardless of—"

JOSH   "—and that's obvious. And it's a beautiful thing to watch,
              to be a party to."

GORDON   "Well, thank you. It's a beautiful thing to live."

JOSH   "I'm sure it is. I know."

GORDON   "But if you have anything to say, well, I'd love to hear it now."

JOSH   My favourite play is *King Lear*. A nice, light comedy. I read it at least once a year. Anyway. There's the scene at the beginning, where Lear is dividing his kingdom in three, based on his daughters' answers. What he's looking for, from his daughters, is for them to make him feel special, to tell him what a great guy he is and why they should get the biggest share of his kingdom. It's similar to what my baba told me once, 'You should tell me why I'm so special.' So King Lear, he gets to the youngest daughter, Cordelia, and she's worried about what to answer and says, 'What shall Cordelia speak? Love, and be silent.' And by being silent when asked she ends up getting nothing. Nothing but banished from the kingdom, banished from her beloved father's sight. Banished. Yet this is what I should speak: 'Love, and be silent.' Take a page from Cordelia's book. *(pause)* Or not. No. Silence didn't do much for my people seventy years ago. No. Speak the truth, look him in the eye and don't blink. Because, because, because it's only politics. It's only politics, right?

GORDON   He's my best friend. I want to think the best of him. Maybe he's just a little jealous. And that's why he hesitated. For not wanting to say anything wrong. But that's what I love about Clotilde. She just says. She just says it. What needs to be said. And I'm trying to be more like her.

              "You're attracted to her."

JOSH   "What?!"

GORDON	"You were staring at her tits."
JOSH	"What are you talking about?"
GORDON	"You were looking at her breasts every chance you could. You're so engorged with jealousy you didn't know what to say!"
JOSH	"Gordon—Gordon—whoa. Wait a second. I might have looked at her chest—okay—it's something I do, I mean.... So I checked her out. I check out women. They're the gender I like. You think about it, it's a compliment. But I'm not jealous; I wasn't staring at her with salacious intent."
GORDON	"Then I don't understand. I don't understand why—"
JOSH	Just tell him the truth.
GORDON	"—why you'd hesitate when I asked—"
JOSH	Tell him and trust, Josh.
GORDON	"—asked because I'm curious—"
JOSH	It's just—it was probably a slip—
GORDON	"—curious about what you thought, and when you wouldn't say—"
JOSH	"Gordon."
GORDON	"Josh."
JOSH	"Okay."

GORDON   "Okay."

JOSH   "We're gonna 'talk' here."

GORDON   "What else would we be doing?"

JOSH   "I understand that. I'm just saying that we're entering a protected zone here, a zone where a couple of dear old friends talk about something without getting too upset."

GORDON   "A safety zone."

JOSH   "Kinda like on *Get Smart* with the cone of silence. Only this is the cone of friendship."

GORDON   "This is making me uneasy, Josh. Why can't you just say it?"

JOSH   But who just says it? Who? Which of us? What would we have to talk about if we actually just said what we thought?

              "I can't just say it because you'll get upset."

GORDON   "So she said something wrong?"

JOSH   "I'm sure she meant no harm."

GORDON   "Josh."

JOSH   "She was talking about that scarf she was wearing—"

GORDON   "You mean the one her mom bought her?"

JOSH   "Yes. And she—"

GORDON	"The scarf she got in Palestine?"
JOSH	The scarf she got in Palestine. Palestine. Palestine. Folks: I'm a Jew.
GORDON	"And?"
JOSH	And? And?
GORDON	"I thought we were going to talk about this."
JOSH	Palestine. I'm looking for peace in the Middle East but as yet there is no Palestine. 1947, the UN granted them their state, two states they said, one Israel, one Palestine. Hey, they think, forget that, why coexist peacefully? Let's start a war instead.
GORDON	"Is there a problem with what she said?"
JOSH	"Well, you know Gord, I'm Jewish."
GORDON	"I hadn't suspected."
JOSH	"And while one prays for peace—"
GORDON	"Do you?"
JOSH	"What?"
GORDON	"Do you pray for peace in the Middle East?"
JOSH	"Well, I hope—"
GORDON	"Do you march for peace?"
JOSH	"March? You mean—"

GORDON   "Organized rallies, where like-minded people—"

JOSH   "I know what a march is. It's the month before April, am I right?"

GORDON   "—like-minded people who show solidarity—"

JOSH   "Hey, I can play solidarity. Just give me a deck of cards and I know lots of variations for solidarity."

GORDON   "We've gone to four demonstrations in the last two months. It's very powerful stuff. Clotilde is quite involved with—"

JOSH   "Now let me ask you this, all kidding aside for a second."

GORDON   "Can you be serious?"

JOSH   "Serious as a heart attack."

GORDON   "Okay."

JOSH   "So you go to these demonstrations."

GORDON   "Yes. A very important part of—"

JOSH   "Sure, exercising a democratic right—"

GORDON   "It's a beautiful thing."

JOSH   "Amen. Whose side, I ask, were you marching on?"

GORDON   "No side."

JOSH   "So you were marching with some Jews?"

GORDON   "I don't know. I didn't ask."

JOSH   "Were you marching with Palestinians?"

GORDON   "Well they're a visible minority, you know, the kaffiyahs, so they're obvious."

JOSH   "Sure. Kaffiyahs, the rifles, the pictures of Sharon as Hitler, no question you marched with Palestinians."

GORDON   "I'm sure there were Jews there."

JOSH   "So you remember seeing some large, hooked noses in retrospect?"

GORDON   "That's offensive."

JOSH   "And saying a scarf is from Palestine isn't?"

GORDON   He's a Jew. I don't mean that badly. *(beat)* I don't think he's a bad person—I love Josh—it's just I've come to realize he doesn't know better. I know why Clotilde said what she did. It was no accident. She wanted to get him thinking.

JOSH   "You don't have a response?"

GORDON   "I'm thinking."

JOSH   "I thought we were talking here."

GORDON   "I'm not allowed to think? Don't you believe one of us should be thinking?"

JOSH   "So I'm not thinking?"

GORDON   "I'm kidding."

JOSH	Most humour is pointed, is a veiled shot. Don't forget that.
GORDON	"Do you believe the Palestinians should have their own state?"
JOSH	"Yes."
GORDON	"Do you think Palestine is a legitimate name for that state?"
JOSH	"Yes."
GORDON	"So why would Clotilde's comment bother you?"
JOSH	Folks, I'm a Jew.
GORDON	He's a Jew.
JOSH	Palestine does not currently exist.
GORDON	He doesn't want it to exist. *(pause)* Maybe.
JOSH	"To say the word today, to give existence to a state that doesn't exist—"
GORDON	"Wasn't the name Israel around for centuries?"
JOSH	"I don't want to get into this."
GORDON	"I think you are into this."
JOSH	"This is causing bad feelings."
GORDON	"It isn't. It isn't. We're two friends just discussing politics. If we can't weather some differences of opinion, what

good would a friendship be that couldn't handle that?"

JOSH   "I don't know."

GORDON   "We've got twelve years history."

JOSH   "I know that."

GORDON   "You're shutting down on me."

JOSH   "Am I?"

GORDON   "You're getting monosyllabic, Joshie."

JOSH   "Is that so?"

GORDON   "We're just dialoging."

JOSH   "Are we?"

GORDON   "That's what we're doing."

JOSH   How difficult is it these days to be a nice, liberal Jew? You can complain about Israel's *(beat)* mistakes, historical and present day. You can say, 'Abolish the settlements, withdraw from the territories, ease all the restrictions now,' but if you remind people it's land-for-peace not give-you-everything-while-you-still-preach-hatred-and-celebrate-suicide-bombers, somehow you're accused of being unreasonable. It's insane.

GORDON   Apologies of the blood. That's what Clotilde calls it. The Jews, the greatest victims of the twentieth century, shifted to the point where they were no longer the oppressed but became the oppressors. Their moral advantage lost, most good-hearts like Josh now stumble in the dark, groping around, excusing Israel's actions with their lack of outrage. Josh explains it away with, 'You don't understand, you're not Jewish.' No. I'm not. And if that precludes understanding, then we don't have a hope, do we?

JOSH   "We're dialoging."

GORDON   "Trying to reach an understanding."

JOSH   "Sorry. I hadn't realized."

GORDON   "I wouldn't be doing this if we weren't friends."

JOSH   "No?"

GORDON   "Of course not. It's because we're friends that we can do this."

JOSH   "Antagonize each other?"

GORDON   "Am I antagonizing you?"

JOSH   "I'm getting a little upset here."

GORDON   "Why? What have I said that's bad?"

JOSH   "You're pushing me, Gord."

GORDON   "Can't friends push each other? When you were nineteen didn't you thank me for giving you a kick in the ass?"

JOSH   "I thanked you because, A, I was nineteen and, B, it had to do with my bizarre obsession with a woman whose nickname was 'The Double Boomer.'"

GORDON   "What was her name again? Sharon... Sharon..."

JOSH   "Flagal."

GORDON   "Sharon 'The Double Boomer' Flagal."

JOSH   "Israel isn't 'The Double Boomer', Gord."

GORDON   "I can't believe you'd get so pissed off over an innocuous comment that Clotilde made over a scarf. That her mother bought her. If she hadn't said it would we even be having this conversation?"

JOSH   "No."

GORDON   "We sat talking for, what, two hours? A few drinks, some nice conversation, and one word gives you doubt about the woman I love? What does that say about you, Josh?"

JOSH   What does that say about me?

GORDON   "If I sat here and made critical remarks about Israel would you take personal offense?"

JOSH   It's a word. One word in thousands that were exchanged. My best friend just wanted me to say, 'I like her, she's great.' What was so tough about that?

GORDON   "Can't we just talk? Can't you summon the respect for someone else's point of view? Especially mine?"

JOSH   "Is it yours?"

GORDON   "What?"

JOSH   "These opinions. This march for peace. I've never known you to do those things."

GORDON   "Yes, I have."

JOSH   "When?"

GORDON   "There was—"

JOSH   "Name once in your life you marched for peace, handed out leaflets for poverty, tell me one time you did something political."

GORDON   *(pause)* "I voted for a socialist once."

JOSH   "Mahatma fucking Gandhi over here. Exactly my point. These issues, the sympathy for the Palestinians—"

GORDON   "—you're saying that's a bad thing?—"

JOSH   "Are you listening to me? Are you listening to me, Gord? What did I tell you before?"

GORDON   "You don't have to get—"

JOSH   "No, I do. I do. I do 'have to get.' Because I told you before I believe in peace. That I desperately want to see peace in the Middle East. I told you I have compassion for what the Palestinians... suffer. So don't imply that I haven't said it or that I don't mean it."

GORDON   "Fine."

JOSH   "My point is this issue, the Palestinians, I know you half my life, and you never raise it once."

GORDON "Maybe because I thought you'd be too sensitive, as you're clearly showing now."

JOSH "You're gonna sit here and lie to my face? Gord? You going to do that? You didn't raise it before, I venture a guess, because you never thought about it."

GORDON "And what are you saying, Josh? Are you saying it's a bad thing that I think of it now?"

JOSH "But you didn't raise the issue, Gord. Because, you ask me, because you could care less. She raised the issue."

GORDON "But she didn't. The point you keep missing in all your righteous anger is that she didn't raise the issue. She simply said 'Palestine.'"

JOSH "And that doesn't raise the issue?"

GORDON "It didn't for her; it did for you. And I still don't know why."

JOSH "She tipped her hand, Gord, she showed all her cards."

GORDON "What are you talking about?"

JOSH "From the back I knew her politics. 'Palestine.' And then you follow it up. 'The East Timorese.' It's the worst of the left these days, the Victim of the Week Club. Or, even better, Victim of the Weak, W-E-A-K. I don't buy it. I don't buy it from anyone."

GORDON "So what are you saying, Josh?"

JOSH "I'm saying I don't believe a word that's coming out of your mouth. I'm saying that this is one of the great acts of ventriloquism I've ever seen: your lips are moving and for the life of me I can't tell that her arm is shoved right up your ass."

I think that might have been overkill. *(pause)* I think I can see small tufts of white smoke coming out of his ears. *(pause)* I don't know how to make this right. And worse, I don't know that I want to.

GORDON   How well do you know anyone? We think, all the time, over and over, we pride ourselves on knowing the people close to us. They say, whoever 'they' are, that you can tell a man by the people he surrounds himself with. Or a woman. The same holds true for them. That goes without saying. Anyway. You can tell about people by who they surround themselves with. Their friends. And we pride ourselves on how well we know our friends. Their goodness. Their constancy. How long we've known them, a quantifiable meaning that lends weight. 'I've known her since I was six.' It tells a story. 'I've known him twelve years.' A weightiness to it. And a hidden meaning: I know them. It's like those friends, the old guard; they're the backbeat in the soundtrack of your life. And then one day they do something or say something so over the top, so cruel, so hateful, that it throws it all into stark relief: How well do I know this person? How well have I ever known them? Can I ever trust this person again? And without trust, how could there ever be true friendship?

JOSH   He can't see it. He can't see that this isn't him. This isn't us, our friendship. Be in love, be happy, just be aware. You got to give up some of who you are to be a couple, right? It's about two individuals coming together to form their own small, unique community. But don't lose sight of yourself. Don't lose your essence.

GORDON So. After those hateful words, what is he going to say now?

JOSH Jesus. What am I going to say now?

GORDON Because I could just up and leave. Go back to the hotel, meet up with Clotilde and let him sit here and won—

JOSH "I'm sorry."

GORDON He's got a ways to go.

JOSH "Gord, I'm sorry. I'm getting, I got ugly there. The hand up the a— I didn't mean it like that."

GORDON "But you meant it?"

JOSH "Why are we doing this to ourselves? Why are we getting ourselves into a knot over a word?"

GORDON "Because it's important."

JOSH "It's important why?"

GORDON "To talk. To participate in democracy. To work out the issues in light of—"

JOSH "Gord, in case you haven't noticed or you've forgotten, I'm not a politician. I'm not a leader of men. And neither, unless you've got a new job over there I don't know about, neither are you."

GORDON "But this is where it begins, Josh. Here. Two people, two friends, talking about the important things in life. The things that touch us. Things. An issue that clearly affects you deeply, shouldn't, mustn't two friends be able to talk about that?"

JOSH   What do people want from me when they raise the
        issue of Israel? Do they want me to confess its sins?
        I do it. In a heartbeat. I show my reasonableness, my
        ability to see past my blood; with a calm, clear mind I
        attempt to differentiate between right and wrong. And
        every time I do it I feel a little sick inside. I feel a little
        defeat. Jews aren't perfect. Israelis aren't perfect. This
        is a revelation to anyone? Why does a friend, why does
        Gordon ask me to denounce my people? Do I ask him
        to denounce his? But, and here's the thing, as a minority,
        how do you get the majority to take blame? Criticize the
        government—'not my government.' Criticize the Pope?
        'I'm no Catholic.' Where's he living now, London? 'I
        just moved there.' They're blameless the accusers. But an
        Israeli is a Jew and a Jew is a Jew, and being a Jew is
        always a dangerous thing.

        "This whole time we've been doing nothing but
        talking."

GORDON "But you became so defensive. Then so aggressive. You're
        confusing me here, Joshie. I'm just talking about free-
        flowing dialogue, an easy exchange."

JOSH   "It ain't free and it clearly ain't easy."

GORDON "But—so—okay, so something was said that sparked
        you, that nudged you, who else you gonna talk about it
        with if not me? I mean, who else is there?"

JOSH   "Your lady said the magic word."

GORDON "Clotilde's fault still?"

JOSH "She said the magic word and the girl wins a prize."

GORDON "And what's the prize? Your wrath?"

JOSH "I was totally friendly towards her."

GORDON "You were civil."

JOSH "Friendly. In spite of being upset."

GORDON "Civil because you were upset."

JOSH "I hugged her goodbye."

GORDON "It was distant."

JOSH "I just met her, Gord."

GORDON "From your body language it's clear you were uncomfortable."

JOSH "I told you I was uncomfortable."

GORDON "Over a word."

JOSH "Over a word."

GORDON "Her mom uses the word, Josh."

JOSH "Her mom."

GORDON "She's an activist. Professionally. It's where Clotilde gets it from."

JOSH "Her mom."

GORDON   "Yeah."

JOSH   "So she's not responsible for what she said."

GORDON   "It was unconscious."

JOSH   "So she's an unconscious anti-Semite."

GORDON   "Crossing a boundary here, Joshie."

JOSH   "Does she know I'm a Jew?"

GORDON   "I'm sure I told her."

JOSH   "So she 'unconsciously' threw out the word Palestine."

GORDON   "It's not like she's sitting there thinking all the time, 'He's a Jew.'"

JOSH   "So she doesn't have the mental wherewithal to think that saying the word 'Palestine' to a Jew might be inflammatory?"

GORDON   "I'm sure that she assumed because you're my best friend that you were on our side."

JOSH   Game, set and match.

"'Our side.'"

GORDON   "Our—that's not what I meant."

JOSH   "'Our side.'"

GORDON   "That you'd agree with our—that you're the type of person who…"

JOSH "Who what? The type of person who—"

GORDON "That's not what I meant."

JOSH "THEN WHY'D YOU SAY IT, GORDON? WHY'D YOU FUCKING SAY IT?"

GORDON We are no longer interested in dialogue. In exploring different opinions. No such thing as anymore. What we seek constantly is the reaffirmation of our beliefs, not a challenge to them. We've become constant litigators in search of our daily bread of proof, proof of what we already know. I lived in that world. At first with blinders on, not able to see anything on the periphery, just what was straight ahead of me. Clotilde was like a jolt of electricity to my brain, she ripped the roof off all my misconceptions, all of my wilful ignorance. I unlearned the myths I was told were truths and found truths where I had never thought to look before. There was only one constant: find the hypocrisy. Expose it. Then blow it up.

Most Americans still cannot accept that years of their imperialistic foreign policy, coupled with governmental support of the most heinous regimes, fomented the hatred that caused the explosions of 9/11. They can't see it because they're too close. In the middle of the Pacific Ocean your only reality is water. Living in Butte, Montana, or wherever, you can't see the dots connect. Living in Europe, in a true multicultural society, you feel the hatred, you speak with the oppressed, you understand causality. Does Josh know that Israel, in its founding war, forcibly expelled over 600,000 Palestinians from their homes and then razed their lands. They enacted racial policies that would make the Nazis blush. Blush. How could these actions lead to anything but the situation the Israelis find themselves in today? Why the suicide bombings? What would you do? Given enough years of oppression, of military aggression, of crippling poverty, of watching innocent children die, your children die—before your eyes—at what point do you say 'Enough! Enough! Strike at me, I'll strike back at you. Kill my children? Fine. I'll kill yours.' Enlightened? No. Understandable. Yes. Connect the dots. That's what I want for Josh. I want him to even see that there are dots.

"Our side, Josh, is humanity. That's our side."

JOSH	"So supporting the Israelis is—is what? Supporting inhumanity?"
GORDON	"They've had inhumane policies."
JOSH	"Suicide bombers are humane?"
GORDON	"They don't represent all Palestinians."
JOSH	"And the Israeli Defense Forces are not all Jews."
GORDON	"I know that. But most Israelis are Jews."
JOSH	He's right. Most of them are. And when a suicide bomber walks into a bus full of Israeli school children and blows them up he's blowing up Jewish children. When Hamas states that they want Israel wiped off the map they want the Jews in Israel wiped off the map. And yet, because we refuse to back down and simply let people kill us any more, we're the most vilified nation in the world. People hate us. They hate us. For no reason other than we're Jews.
GORDON	"We're talking about historical decisions dating back to

the very formation of Israel. If you read as closely as
I've read—"

JOSH "I just want to be clear of something here for a
second."

GORDON "Sure. What?"

JOSH "We're just 'talking' here."

GORDON "Isn't that the idea?"

JOSH "A couple of friends exchanging political beliefs,
right?"

GORDON "To expose ourselves to—to different ideas. Listen,
I'm not mad that you didn't like Clotilde—"

JOSH "I liked her. I didn't like what she said."

GORDON "And we're trying to get to the root of your upset."

JOSH "The 'root' of."

GORDON "You are my dearest friend."

JOSH "Now that's an astonishing thing to hear."

GORDON "Josh, how could you ever doubt?"

JOSH "Simple: I'm listening to what you're saying to me—"

GORDON "One conversation in the course of twelve years. It's
like the one word you focused on of Clotilde's in the
two hours that you've known her. Proportionality, Josh.
Put things into context. This political exchange, it's just

words. Don't lose sight of that. These are just words."

JOSH   "I don't think they're just words."

GORDON   "Of course they are. What else could they be?"

JOSH   "They're beliefs."

GORDON   "Beliefs."

JOSH   "It's what we're made of. What we believe, Gord."

GORDON   "So it means something to you that I have a different belief?"

JOSH   "On this one, yes."

GORDON   "Why? Because you're a Jew?"

JOSH   I worked with this woman once. Nice lady, not a prejudiced bone in her body. Sweet as a freshly baked chocolate-chip cookie. We're talking about this, that, whatever, and I say, 'You know, of course I love Chinese food, I'm a Jew.' And she says, 'Don't say that word.' I'm like, 'What word?' She says, 'Jew.' I ask why. She says she finds it offensive. She finds it offensive. Jew. I ask her what should I say so as not to disturb her delicate sensibilities. She says, 'Jewish. Say you're Jewish. It's not so offensive that way. Not so harsh.'

"Because I'm a Jew."

GORDON   "I just don't understand why we can't have a talk about this."

JOSH   "Because I'm getting deeply offended. Because you're moving past the point of a friendly debate into something personal."

GORDON   "But you're not an Israeli."

JOSH   "Have you taken a stupid pill? I'm happy you love this woman, I hope her very sight causes you more pleasure than you've ever had, but you're leading me to the conclusion you've lost your mind."

GORDON   "Because I asked you if you were Israeli?"

JOSH   "Listen, if it was 1936 would you tell me not to take offence at Hitler because I wasn't living in Germany?"

GORDON   "You're missing the point."

JOSH   "You don't even know that the point is. What is your point? What do you want from this conversation, Gord?"

GORDON   "I... I want..." *(pause)*

JOSH   He doesn't know. And there you have it, folks. He's so far into an aggressive mode to make me admit something about my being Jewish, that it's suddenly offensive to him because his new lady is an activist, or she's sitting there feeding him the latest distortion about the Middle E—

GORDON   "I want to know why you had to bring up the fact that Clotilde said Palestine. Why you couldn't have kept your mouth shut. Because I want to know why your Jewishness was more important to this evening than our friendship. All I wanted from tonight was for you to meet Clotilde."

JOSH   "Well, that happened."

GORDON   "It's not funny, Josh."

JOSH   "Sorry."

GORDON   "So she said something you found offensive. So what? What would it have cost you to bite your lip? To bury your thoughts? Why did I need to know that you were offended?"

JOSH   "Because I can tell you anything."

GORDON   "If that's the case then why do you have a double standard when it comes to me?"

He, of course, doesn't see it. He doesn't see his own casual, cloaked-in-humour racism. He kiddingly calls me a goy, a gimmel (the Hebrew letter that begins the word goy), a shegitz (Yiddish for a Gentile male). He calls Jews goys and says this designates them as stupid but doesn't mean that Gentiles are stupid, though clearly that's his equation. And the word goy in the Bible means 'other nations.' Other. Does Josh hate me? No. He loves me. Not because I'm not Jewish but in spite of it. This is the block he has towards the Palestinians. Josh can love Gentiles. Why? Because he knows them. He's interacted with them. Are there some anti-Semitic assholes out there? Too many. But he knows what he's dealing with and in what measure. I guarantee you he's never spoken with a Palestinian. He's never been exposed to their inherent beauty, a beautiful people. They want a land of their own, a state of their own. The same dream that drove Theodor Herzl in the early days of Zionism. They want to share the land. They can't compete with Israel militarily; it's not David versus Goliath, it's a gun versus a tank—the tank will always win. And because he doesn't know, he hates. The very disease, ignorance, that fuels anti-Semitism is the force he's allowing to drive us apart. And he doesn't see it. He's as blind as a bat.

JOSH   It took him all night but he finally scored a point. If I can say anything to him why can't he say anything to me? If I told him I was offended by the Palestine remarks why shouldn't he be able to challenge me on the reasons of my offence? *(pause)* But he has. I never told him to stop, I simply warned him we were traversing slippery ground, someone could get hurt. And now he's hurt because I've rightly called him an idiot and he's hiding behind—

"What double standard? Think, Gord, think. I told you what was up because you hammered me on it, told you the truth as you requested. You got offended by what I said, attacked me because you don't like my views on the occupied territories—"

GORDON   "So you admit they're occupied?"

JOSH   "If they were unoccupied this would be a pretty stupid argument, wouldn't it?"

GORDON   "Just want to make sure we're on the same page here."

JOSH   "But we are not, we are fundamentally not, Gord. You accuse me of a double standard, which I don't have, just because you don't like my answers. That's not the same page, we're not even in the same book."

GORDON   "But you have a double standard, Josh. You're a hypocrite because you say I'm not allowed to be upset when you falsely accuse my—"

JOSH   "Falsely? Falsely? Did she or did she not say Palestine?"

GORDON   "You let me talk for a second without interrupting me you might actually hear what I'm saying."

JOSH   "Talk."

GORDON   "You say I'm not allowed to be upset when you call—"

JOSH   "So it's call now, not 'falsely accuse.' *(beat)* I'm listening. Talk."

GORDON   "You accuse my fiancée—"

JOSH   "Whoa, whoa, whoa. Stop all this other shit. I'm sorry. Fiancée? Fiancée, Gord? What are you—you never told me that."

GORDON   "I thought you would have figured it out."

JOSH   "I didn't see a ring. I looked. I half expected but I didn't see one. I'm not a mind reader. Gord. Come on. You're engaged to be married? *(pause)* You actually ask her yet?"

GORDON   "Not yet but it's a formality."

JOSH   "So you find it necessary, I guess, to ratchet up the emotional deck against me with something that hasn't happened yet. Could the two of you exhibit a little patience before you speak?"

GORDON   "Why don't you listen to the essence of what I'm saying?"

JOSH   "'Cause all you got are words, Gord, that's all any of us got."

GORDON   "I'm trying to make a point here. You accuse my fiancée-to-be of being anti-Semitic and I'm not allowed to be angry by your reasoning, yet you're fully justified in your upset because she said the word Palestine? Something's really, really wrong here, Josh. And I think it's you."

JOSH   Palestine. The word came into existence around 135 Common Era, after the Romans rid that land of the Jews yet again. The biblical names Judea and Samaria were abolished and the land was renamed Palestine. After the Philistines. True. Dictionary definition of the word Philistine? 'A crass, prosaic, often priggish individual guided by material rather than intellectual values.' You can't make this up.

"You know what's wrong? What's wrong is you just sat there blinking blindly while your lady laid this on me. Not a peep. Not even a double take from you."

GORDON   "You didn't say anything."

JOSH   "I was too shocked. 'Palestine.' I didn't realize I was having martinis with Arafat. You might also realize I was trying to keep things civil so we could have a nice evening."

GORDON   "You had balls you would have said something."

JOSH   "You had balls so would you."

GORDON   All this from a simple question.

JOSH   All this from 'So what do you think of her?'

GORDON   I could have asked a different question.

JOSH   I could have said something different.

GORDON   Was all this necessary?

JOSH   Could'a gone different.

GORDON   Should'a gone different.

JOSH   What if?

GORDON   It's a simple question…

> *Lights change. The actors resume their positions from the beginning of the play.*

"So what do you think of her?"

JOSH   "What do I think of her?"

GORDON   "Yeah. What do you think of her?"

JOSH   *(pause)* "I like her."

GORDON   "You like her."

JOSH   "I really like her, Gord."

GORDON   "Can I ask why?"

JOSH   "What is this, a quiz?"

GORDON   "I'm—I'm—I'm excited that you like her, that's all, I want to know why, to share—"

JOSH   "She's great, Gord, she's, let's face it, she's beautiful, she's bright, very well-informed about things, interesting mind, she's engaging, she—"

GORDON "Hey, whoa, whoa, whoa, she's my lady here, Joshie."

JOSH "Hey, listen, she's crazy about you, I'm thrilled and shocked she even noticed I was in the room."

GORDON "Ah, Jesus, she liked you, Josh, you could tell, maybe, she can occasionally be a bit shy."

JOSH "She's shy?"

GORDON "No, really, yeah, around new people she can be, but she just warmed to you because—"

JOSH "She's a great lady, Gord."

GORDON "I'm—I'm so happy, I am so happy I can't begin to tell you."

JOSH "You deserve this happiness."

GORDON "Well, well, thank you. I do, you know, you're right about that, and so do you."

JOSH "I know. And in time I will."

And it goes like that.

GORDON Just like that.

JOSH And it's great.

GORDON It is. It's a—it's a—

JOSH It's what it's all about.

GORDON   It is.

JOSH   We down a few more Scotches, the good stuff now, eighteen-year-olds, and ain't that a fine age—

GORDON   And we slap each other on the back, laugh too hard, say how good it is to see each other.

JOSH   And it is.

GORDON   It is.

JOSH   We carefully weave our separated fabrics back together, catch up on this complicated mess we call life.

GORDON   We say goodnight.

JOSH   *(They hug.)* "Goodnight, man."

GORDON   "Goodnight."

JOSH   And in that hug is everything that a million words could never express to others about our friendship.

GORDON   Not even to Clotilde.

JOSH   But we get it.

GORDON   I go back to the hotel to hook up with Clotilde. I'm so incredibly happy. I tell her, 'Baby, I'm so happy.'

JOSH   And they shtup like happy little bunnies.

GORDON   Clotilde gets drunk on my enthusiasm, and isn't life, aren't people, isn't it all just a wondrous thing?

JOSH	I go home to my apartment. As I enter the phone is ringing. It's my buddy Abe. I tell him about Gord and the little lady.
GORDON	"And what do you tell him?"
JOSH	I tell him it was great.
GORDON	And it was.
JOSH	And it was. But I do tell Abe about her. About the scarf she was wearing. About the Palestine comment.
GORDON	As I lie in bed beside Clotilde, in a state of such perfect elation that I almost can't understand it, I think back to this great night and I hope Josh is falling asleep with a grin on his face too.
JOSH	Abe agrees her comment's a little weird. But we make jokes about it, our typical Jewish response. It's no big deal. I see Gord again towards the end of his trip.
GORDON	We have lunch.
JOSH	We eat.
GORDON	We say goodbye.
JOSH	"So I guess this is it. All good lunches must come to an end."
GORDON	"It was great to see you."
JOSH	"And you, my friend. A shame your girlfriend couldn't join us."

GORDON   "Yeah. She said there were some things she wanted to do and I guess she didn't finish in time to join us."

JOSH   "Things to do?"

GORDON   "Yeah."

JOSH   "Here?"

GORDON   "Yeah."

JOSH   "Sure. Understandable. Given that she's only ever lived in Paris and London, I imagine Winnipeg must be a real shot of excitement. I mean, really, can you beat Polo Park for architectural splendour?"

GORDON   "She wanted to give us some alone time."

JOSH   "And have that we did."

GORDON   And we don't say another word about it.

JOSH   And I never stopped wondering about it.

GORDON   I head back to London.

JOSH   We talk.

GORDON   We email.

JOSH   The usual stuff.

GORDON   It's good.

JOSH   Gord's good.

GORDON   I'm great.

JOSH   I'm fine.

GORDON   Josh's great.

JOSH   I'm fine.

GORDON   It's the usual.

JOSH   It's our friendship.

GORDON   It never changes.

JOSH   It slightly changes.

GORDON   It's still our friendship.

JOSH   It is that.

GORDON   And six months later, I've got news.

            "Man, have I got news."

JOSH   "So tell me."

GORDON   "You've got to guess."

JOSH   (beat) "You're getting married."

GORDON   "How did you know?"

JOSH   "It was either that or you won the lottery, and you
            don't sound nearly excited enough for that."

GORDON   "You're hilarious."

JOSH	"Hey, fifty million—"
GORDON	"Chinese, I know, I know."
JOSH	"This is amazing news, Gordon. I'm thrilled for you."
GORDON	"We're gonna have it in the south of France."
JOSH	"You know I'll be there."
GORDON	"Of course you'll be there. You're the best man."
JOSH	"I'm honoured."
GORDON	"I don't care if you are or not, you're still the best man."
JOSH	And I'm thrilled because it's one of these things you think about. Standing up for a friend. To be at his side at the happiest moment of his life. It's everything I've ever wanted for Gordon.
GORDON	I want the simplest of things: Happiness, love. I want simplicity. I've overcomplicated things in the past. I clouded my head with too many thoughts. This is simple: Marrying Clotilde with Josh as my best man. It's simple and it makes me happy.
JOSH	But there's a pit. In my stomach. A qualm. But this is my friend, one of my best friends we're talking about here, and this is not about a premonition, if that's what it is I'm having, and I've mostly forgotten about what she said. And how she didn't show for lunch. I've forgotten. Mostly. *(beat)* I have to remember to forget.
GORDON	I tell Clotilde about my family, my friends, stories she's

heard before, but I tell them again and she indulges me. I tell her a story about Josh, the two of us, of a memory I can't shake. Do you remember?

JOSH   "You're going to say—"

GORDON   Banff.

JOSH   Yes, Banff.

GORDON   The back seat of the rental car. Susie's driving.

JOSH   Ellen in the passenger seat. Girls up front, boys in the back.

GORDON   Just watching the scenery, driving to Jasper. It's so beautiful.

JOSH   It is. It's stunning.

GORDON   *Automatic for the People* by R.E.M. playing on the radio.

JOSH   "Nightswimming" is the song I remember.

Josh sings two or three lines from the song.

GORDON   And we're not saying a word.

JOSH   Don't have to. We're just watching out the window.

GORDON   Just watching.

JOSH   Happy times.

GORDON   Happy times, yes. A kind of bliss. Clotilde squeezes my hand when I finish this story. She's happy for me. Images swarm my head, so many of them, how the varying parts of my life will all merge. How my life in London and my love from London, my present and future, will be combined with my friends and family, my past and future, and I see that love we have bouncing around like a crazed puppy. I want them to share in my joy, to have joy for my joy, and I want to rejoice in the joy they have for my joy. It's an endless wedding cake and I don't want to stop eating.

And I tell her about Josh again, and the history of our friendship yet again, because he's the one who's known me best, the one who's been there in the past, the one who— *(beat)* And I pause because I can't quite explain the bond, not fully, it's there though, it's something she'll have to see to understand. And I tell her, I tell her the great thing about Josh, our hallmark, is that we're able to discuss anything. That's why he's here. That's why he's my best man.

And I can see the excitement in his eyes when we finally pull up to Clotilde's place in the south of France. He doesn't have to say it. But he does.

JOSH   "This is paradise."

GORDON   "Think it's nice?"

JOSH   "It's a... Jesus, and you say she's good in bed? Fuck you."

GORDON   "Nice digs, huh."

JOSH   "Gorgeous digs."

GORDON   "Kind of makes a man want to stay here or something, huh?"

JOSH   "No shit."

GORDON   "Clotilde's thrilled that you're here.... Honey!"

JOSH   And there she is. She looks great. The very definition of a glowing bride.

GORDON   I make sure the three of us spend time together. They need to really bond this time.

JOSH   I spend time with the two of them. Best man privileges and all. While her English has improved lots, I think that the more she learns the language the less I like her. There's an edge to her, it makes my teeth hurt. There's a prickliness, like she's the barbed wire gone up around Gordo to keep him safe. Or to keep him to herself. As their day approaches Gordo and I get more alone time. I appreciate it for all sorts of reasons. We're drinking late one night when Gordo says:

GORDON   "Hey, question for you."

JOSH   "Sure."

GORDON   "It isn't a problem for you that we're getting married in a church, is it?"

JOSH   "Why would it be a problem?"

GORDON   "I don't know."

JOSH   "Are you worried I'm going to start speaking Hebrew in tongues or something?"

GORDON   "No."

JOSH   "It'd be pretty cool if I did considering I don't even
           know the language."

GORDON   "I was just checking."

JOSH   Being considerate. Is he so sensitive about being
           Jewish?

           It's such a weird question. And I know Gordon would
           have never thought to ask it. Why would it be a problem
           for me? Is it a problem for them?

GORDON   Josh's different now. He's changed. He looks older, I
           know, strange to say at our age, but he does. He's got
           these bags around his eyes now, they're there constantly.
           He's got some grey hairs. He's put on weight too, just
           enough that it shows—or that I notice. And he calls me
           Gordo now, all the time, like:

JOSH   "Hey Gordo, do you have any sugar for this coffee?"

GORDON   Or:

JOSH   "Hey Gordo, what's the French word for fart?"

GORDON   He's never called me Gordo. Ever. And he's withdrawn.
           The night after the wedding there's a family function
           and he knows he's part of the family now but he won't
           come. I ask him why. He says:

JOSH   "I'm just tired, that's all."

GORDON   "It's just dinner, Joshie."

JOSH   "I'll just stay here, cool my heels, I may be getting sick, still adjusting to the time difference."

GORDON   "Just in time for you to go home."

JOSH   "Yeah."

GORDON   "You'll be missed."

JOSH   "Send my regrets."

It's been a good trip. But I'm ready to go home. They go out for their family function. I go through their bookshelves. I've wanted to do it since I first arrived; always my first inclination when I go to someone's home, see what books they're reading, what music they're listening to. I'm looking with intent this time. I look through the books—to no avail as they're all in French. But from what I can tell there's no copy of *Protocols of the Elders of Zion* and no copy of *Mein Kampf* with notes in the margin that read 'Good idea!' So that's a relief. Maybe I've been uncomfortable for the wrong reasons.

GORDON   It hits me the next day as we're driving to the airport that maybe Josh's just been jet-lagged all this time. And that's all.

JOSH   "This was tremendous."

GORDON   "This was unbelievable. I can't begin to—you were my right hand, my right arm. If you weren't here I don't know what I would have done."

JOSH   "You would have said 'I do' and things would have worked out just fine."

GORDON   "I love you, man."

JOSH   "I love you."

GORDON   And I do.

JOSH   And I do.

GORDON   And life goes on.

JOSH   It always does.

GORDON   And time passes.

JOSH   As it must.

GORDON   And six months later I tell Joshie the news: "We're moving to France!"

JOSH   "To France? I thought you loved London."

GORDON   "I do but I love France too. The people are incredible, Josh. You met them."

JOSH   "It's her country."

GORDON   "Yeah."

JOSH   "Her friends."

GORDON   "They're my friends—"

JOSH   "Her family."

GORDON   "Well of course."

JOSH	"Her history."
GORDON	"It's not like I'm a member of the House of Lords."
JOSH	"Her language."
GORDON	"Hey, I still have trouble with English. Listen, this was important to Clotilde so there was no question. These are the decisions you learn to make, Josh. What's important for the greater good. I'm going to learn so much. This is going to be an amazing adventure."
JOSH	"I'm happy for you."
GORDON	He isn't.
JOSH	I'm not.
GORDON	But I'm happy.
JOSH	That's what I read in his emails. He's happy now. He doesn't phone now, only emails. Some set-up where they only have a cell phone in France and to call overseas it—I don't know—not allowed, or expensive, whatever. He writes about how much she continues to teach him. Especially politically. The atrocities that took place in his backyard that he never knew about. How could he have been so blind? So ignorant? What, his parents mass-murdered kittens and he just found out about it?
GORDON	I see the world in a new light. Hell, I see the world. For the first time. It's not a pretty sight. There's work to be done. A revolution of thought, Clotilde calls it. It's a nice phrase. One day I email these great articles to Josh so he can understand my thinking better.

JOSH   To further articulate the influences on his thinking, he writes. This is a brand new world, he adds, so it requires brand new thinking. Okay, and so I read the articles. All the tepid, facile arguments of the Left that blame the terrorist attacks on US foreign policy. The articles, and Gordon, are making apologies for Bin Laden. Are you kidding me? It's the same thing as saying a rape victim deserved it because she dressed provocatively or saying that the Jews in the Holocaust somehow deserved it. I have no patience for this stupidity. And in one of the articles the author lists a series of atrocities, stating how sad each one made him, how sickened he felt upon hearing the news. There's litany upon litany railing against Israel, all of her crimes, every last error a heart-wringing tragedy for the author with nary a mention of a single Palestinian fault. And I wonder what could make one of my best friends send me such an article. He knows I have to respond. I have to say 'Gordo, this is unacceptable, you cannot send me anti-Semitic articles.' And I do. I tell him to read across the political spectrum. Get a balanced view. He writes back. Huffy, seriously pissed off, how dare I diminish his opinions or not respect them? Easy. They're STUPID. He defends the articles, he defends his reading of them and he lets a little tidbit slip:

GORDON   My reading is balanced. Clotilde does an excellent job of translating a whole range of articles for me.

JOSH   And game, set, match. He doesn't see it: she's choosing what he reads.

GORDON   He doesn't see it. I just—I'm trying to communicate with him, that's all, let him know where I'm coming from, open up a little dialogue, a little political talk with my best friend. Out of fourteen pages of articles

he focuses in on one section, a few paragraphs, he's
enraged about Israel, enraged I would read something
that would dare criticize Israel, like there's an entire
context being pointed out to him that he can't see. And
I'm sure he think it's Clotilde, I'm sure he blames her,
somewhere in his heart, when all she's doing, all I'm
doing with her, is exchanging ideas. Thinking things
out. Jesus Christ, we're thinking. Trying to understand
this muddle of a world and we're working at it together.
And I feel for Josh almost, knowing that he's adrift on
this one, alone, out there, and he can't see past his own
prejudices, his own blood. He can't see his old friend is
just reaching out to him.

JOSH   If I am attacked as a Jew I will defend myself as a Jew.
              (beat) I cannot compete against this woman. And I don't
              want to. What I want I can't have. I want my old friend
              back. The one who didn't send me subtle hate mail. The
              one who lived his life. And he's gone. To a better place?
              Maybe. He thinks so. I don't but what do I know? He
              says he's happy. *Zei gezundt.*

GORDON   It isn't this exchange that does us in though. I'll write
              something or do something or not do something, he'll
              find something to latch onto, I'll be in the wrong no
              matter what. I can't help but lose. It'll be Clotilde's fault.
              You watch. He'll blame Clotilde.

JOSH   It isn't this exchange that does us in though. I'll write
              something or do something or not do something, he'll
              find something to latch onto, I'll be in the wrong no
              matter what. I can't help but lose. I'll be banished
              summarily, righteously, angrily. How I've betrayed him.

              *Lighting changes. The actors resume their previous position
              from page 38.*

"You know what's wrong? What's wrong is you just sat there blinking blindly while your lady laid this on me. Not a peep. Not even a double take from you."

GORDON   "You didn't say anything."

JOSH   "I was too shocked. 'Palestine.' I didn't realize I was having martinis with Arafat. You might also realize I was trying to keep things civil so we could have a nice evening."

GORDON   "If you had balls you would have said something."

JOSH   "So is this what you would have wanted? Your lady says the bit about Palestine. And what I should have said: 'And where exactly is Palestine?' 'Cause I think I know maps and atlases pretty well and I'd swear there's no such place. Unless you're referring to those textbooks they use in Palestinian schools where they teach their kids that Israel doesn't exist. What? Then we're gonna sit around and talk about old times? She'd leave in a huff, you'd leave in a minute and a huff. And I'd get blamed for ruining the evening, I'd get blamed for being confrontational. I would be assailed for being oversensitive. How could I? And then what? We're gonna remain best buds? My guess is I'd be hearing about your wedding through mutual friends and I'd still hear years later how pissed off you are with me. Because I talked back. Because I had the temerity to bring up the point that I find people who kill Jews as a form of protest unconscionable. And it's never acknowledged that she raised the subject. That doesn't matter. What matters is I stuck up for myself, I stuck up for Jews. And that, in the end, is unforgivable. Is that what you really would have wanted?"

GORDON   "You're so far gone it isn't funny."

JOSH   "So I'm the one who's screwed up."

GORDON   "Yes you are, my friend."

JOSH   "And you're blameless, of course."

GORDON   "I don't think I've dumped on your parade."

JOSH   "Right past pissing on it to crapping all over it?"

GORDON   "Big steaming piles of it."

JOSH   "So what do you want, Gordon?"

GORDON   "I want you to apologize for ruining the evening."

JOSH   "I want to be clear: I ruined it."

GORDON   "Yes."

JOSH   "This is all my doing?"

GORDON   "You had a choice. You chose your self-righteousness over my simple need for a nice evening."

JOSH   "A nice evening."

GORDON   "That's all I wanted."

JOSH   "I thought that's what we had, at least it was until she left."

GORDON   "I thought she was the problem."

JOSH	"Was she? Things were fine up until she left."
GORDON	"But she said something that shook your soul."
JOSH	"It didn't shake my soul. It upset me. So I told you. And then the 'nice' evening got shot to hell."
GORDON	"So if Clotilde had stayed, you're now saying, none of this would have happened?"
JOSH	"I don't know that."
GORDON	"I do."
JOSH	"You do?"
GORDON	"Yes. I do. You've changed, Josh. Since I last saw you. You've changed."
JOSH	"I should hope so."
GORDON	"Not for the better though."
JOSH	"Not the better."
GORDON	"No."
JOSH	"Well... thanks for the compliment."
GORDON	"You're too oversensitive. I don't know what's happened. Tonight. It was just a word."
JOSH	"They were all just words, Gord. Every last one of them."
GORDON	"You let me down tonight, Josh. This wasn't about you."

JOSH   "Sorry. Next time I'm attacked I'll try not to notice."

GORDON   "Must everything you say be sarcastic?"

JOSH   (beat) "Yes."

GORDON   "You used to be funny."

JOSH   "You used to have a sense of humour."

GORDON   "You used to be funny."

JOSH   "You used to have a sense of humour."

I don't understand how we've gotten here. Not quite. I know with each sentence, with each word now, we make things worse. More complicated. We entrench our positions further. We've moved into some bizarre twilight where things have changed forever. It's like a screw that loses its thread; permanently useless. It reminds me of, you know, the whole thing about the Second Intifada. I got into an argument once with someone about it, how the Palestinians were riled and provoked by Sharon's offensive action. The man went for a walk. He went for a goddamned walk and that was justification for killing Jews? Have we lost our minds?

Gordon and I stand in what seems like an eternity of silence. I don't know why, perhaps it's an old habit, perhaps because love should conquer all, and I've got nothing to lose and everything to gain. One for the Gipper, right?

"I'm sorry you're hurt, Gordon. I'm sorry you're so upset. I truly am."

GORDON   But— *(beat)* But he's not sorry for what's he done. For what he's done. And he can't see how tragically this underscores the whole debate we've just had, the whole problem with the Palestinians and the Jews. The Jews are genuinely sorry that their soldiers were firing at targets in the territories and that they accidentally killed a child, they're sorry about that. But they're not sorry that they're in the territories to begin with. If they were, if they admitted they were wrong in the first place, then maybe you have a chance at true dialogue. Maybe you have a chance at peace. At a revolutionary change. For the betterment of the world. Josh's sorry I'm upset but unrepentant for the actions that got us to this point.

          "Well I appreciate the apology."

JOSH   "Do you?"

GORDON   "Yes. I do."

JOSH   And at this point it's lies, lies, all lies, all the time. It doesn't matter to him if I'm truly sorry, it only matters that I remain wrong. I refuse to say 'You're right about everything.' I can't have my minority opinion, I can't tell him he's gone insane. It's acquiesce or else.

          "And are you sorry?"

GORDON   No.

          "Yes."

JOSH   He's not.

GORDON   He knows I'm not.

JOSH

And I'm left to wonder what sort of friend would attack your beliefs?

GORDON

And I'm left to wonder what sort of friend would attack your beliefs?

JOSH

This is one of those moments, as we fumble for the right exit words, the ones we can both live with, this is a moment when you know your life is changing permanently and it's your last look backwards at the way things have been. And do you look back and try to salvage the past or embrace the unknown future? What do you do?

"So, uh, yeah. So. *(beat)* So we're both sorry."

GORDON

"Yeah."

JOSH

"And here we are."

GORDON

"Yeah. *(beat)* I've got to, I should go, to meet Clotilde, back at the… I'm sure she's expecting me."

JOSH

"Well she's not expecting me."

GORDON

"No, that's true. That'd be a bit of a surprise, you showed up."

JOSH

"I think I should. You know? Tell her that we talked about it some after she left—"

GORDON

"—that's right—"

JOSH

"Decided after a few drinks, might be best for all involved if we switched things up, trade places for a while."

GORDON   "Absolt-ly."

JOSH   "Yes, absolt-ly. Because we figured a little variety being the spice of life and all."

GORDON   "Some crushed red pepper flakes on vanilla ice cream."

JOSH   "Really? You into that?"

GORDON   "You never know what a person's into."

JOSH   "Ain't that the truth. We'll tell her it's just temporary though."

GORDON   "Of course. Just a, you know—"

JOSH   "Temporary thing."

GORDON   "That would pass."

JOSH   "Yeah. Enjoy it as a stroll in the park type thing."

GORDON   "Because it's not like you'd be right for her."

JOSH   "No. *(beat)* No. Because it's clear—"

GORDON   "—yeah, yeah—"

JOSH   "—that you are."

GORDON   "That much is obvious."

JOSH   "Clear as day. *(beat)* So I guess it'll be a busy week."

GORDON   "Yeah. A lot of family stuff. As you can imagine. Got to do the drive to go see the folks."

JOSH	"Naturally. A busy bee."
GORDON	"Very."
JOSH	"And out of town. Lovely Victoria Beach."
GORDON	"For most of it."
JOSH	"Goes without saying, which is why I almost didn't say it. Couldn't help myself though."
GORDON	"You never can. *(beat)* They're anxious to meet Clotilde."
JOSH	"Future daughter-in-law they figure, can you blame them?"
GORDON	"No. I guess I'm nervous about it."
JOSH	"Don't be. They'll love her."
GORDON	"Will they?"
JOSH	"Your folks?"
GORDON	"Yeah."
JOSH	"They'll eat her up. Your mother? Katy, bar the door. Sheila's losing her mind over your bride to be. Couldn't be happier."
GORDON	"You're probably right."
JOSH	"On this one, you can give me credit, I'm right. *(beat)* You'll say hello for me. To your folks."
GORDON	*(beat)* "Sure. I'm sure they'll say hello back."

JOSH   "Can I ask you something?"

GORDON   "Dealer's choice."

JOSH   "You believe everything you said tonight?"

GORDON   "Do you?"

JOSH   "Yes."

GORDON   "So you expect my answer to be any different?"

JOSH   "It's a shame, you know."

GORDON   "What is?"

JOSH   "You not being around this week."

GORDON   "Why?"

JOSH   "There's this Jewish singles event on Christmas Eve. Could have been a blast."

GORDON   "Wouldn't I have triggered the goy alarm?"

JOSH   "You could have been my wingman, vouched on my credentials as Christ Killer. Chicks dig that stuff."

GORDON   "You're an asshole, you know that?"

JOSH   "Fifty million Chinese can't be wrong."

GORDON   "I've been hearing this expression the last twelve years of my life. What does it mean?"

JOSH   "How should I know? It's just something I say."

Beat.

GORDON   "I really should get going."

JOSH   "Before you do."

GORDON   "What?"

JOSH   "You remember… remember what you said to me? Twelve years ago in the hallway of U of W , Bryce Hall, first conversation we ever had, you remember what you said to me?"

GORDON   "I don't have a clue."

JOSH   *(beat)* "Neither do I."

He said, 'Hey, you, you play poker?' I didn't but of course I said I did. And I played. And Gordon was great, so lovely. I warmed to him instantly. Not, not my usual type of friend, you understand, he wasn't a great speaker, not a great volleyer of insults and banter, but his goodness, his heart, I could spot those qualities a mile away. And about a year after that first invitation, when I knew he was going to be one of those people who would be around for the rest of my life, I brought up the subject again, our first fateful conversation, I asked him why he invited me, some schmuck just standing in the hallway, to his exclusive poker game. And he said:

GORDON   "I don't know. I just wanted to."

JOSH   And I told him a line from *King Lear*, 'You have that in your countenance which I would fain call friend.' And I told him he could bank on that. For life.

GORDON   It's two years later. A typical, rainy French November
          day. I'm a volunteer at an old-folk's home in town. I
          spend three hours each week reading to a group of
          them, occasionally they get me to play cards with
          them. I've got a great evening ahead, Clotilde's made
          plans for us with her friends Alain and Sondrine, great
          people, they've treated me like one of their own from
          moment go. I'm finishing up a game of poker I've been
          playing with Mister Abrams, a nice man originally from
          Florida. He's taken a shine to me and I sneak him some
          chocolate-chip cookies, which he's not supposed to
          eat, but I can't find a way to refuse him. I've won today,
          hands down, winning well over sixty hard candies from
          him, which has left Mister Abrams none too happy. As
          I'm leaving he asks me for my phone number. And I ask
          why. And he says, 'In case I should die, I can call.'

          And in his voice, in his rhythm, I can hear my old friend.
          Abrams, it's a Jewish name and I probably knew it all
          along. And I wonder if that's part of the reason I like
          him so much.

          And then my cell phone rings. It's Clotilde. And it's
          time to go.

JOSH   It's two years later. A typical Winnipeg winter day. Well
          a typical old-school Winnipeg winter day, negative forty,
          sunny and the only place you're going is from the living
          room to the kitchen and back. So, nothing to do, I sit
          down and decide to reread *King Lear*. I know—I need to
          get a life, a girlfriend at very least. Anyway. I'm reading,
          I come across the line I said to Gordon all those years
          ago. 'You have that in your countenance which I would
          fain call friend.' Except. That's not the line. I got the line
          wrong. It's not friend, its master. 'You have that in your
          countenance which I would fain call master.' I couldn't

call anyone master, I couldn't give over my thoughts, my actions, to another person. Ever. It doesn't work well for us Jews.

I finish reading the play. I think about Cordelia, who could not lie, would not flatter the king's ego and paid for her banishment with her life. I could hang with that sort of woman. I take out a pack of cards, play some solitaire and take comfort that it will be warm again some day.

END

ACKNOWLEDGEMENTS

A LOT OF PEOPLE are responsible for this play seeing the light of day. My father, Sidney, who inculcated my love of theatre, which helped lead me to this place. My thanks to Carol Matas and my beloved wife, Rebecca Brask, who heard the first draft and provided great feedback. This play has been championed for years by Vern Thiessen, in whose debt I remain. My thanks to Rory Runnells and the Manitoba Association of Playwrights who made sure *Talk* got into the right hands and helped with critically important readings and workshops. My thanks to Graham Ashmore and Chris Sabel for their workshop contributions. A huge thanks to Mariam Bernstein, former Artistic Director of WJT (Winnipeg Jewish Theatre) for having the faith and trust to program this play. A special thank you to Ross McMillan, Michael Rubenfeld and Matthew TenBruggencate, the director and actors who both workshopped and created the original production of *Talk*. They improved the text and made it resonate with deep beauty. And last but not least, my thanks to my long-time dramaturg and current multi-hyphenate Per Brask, who has always pushed me as a writer and kept me moving forward.

photo by Steve Salnikowski

MICHAEL NATHANSON BEGAN HIS career acting on television at age thirteen. More recently, his focus has been on writing. As a playwright Michael's work has been seen in New York (LaMaMa Etc.), Dallas (Kitchen Dog Theatre) and at festivals across Canada (Montreal, Toronto, Edmonton and Vancouver). At home, Michael has written for Theatre Projects Manitoba (*To Kill the Weatherman*), CBC radio (*Past/Present*) and the University of Winnipeg (*City of Destiny, No Offense*). In the past few years he also created and wrote two original, animated, fifty-episode internet-based series for Little Fox, Korea.

As a director, credits include: *Little Ease* (West End Cultural Centre), *Right For It* (Voices From The West), *To Kill the Weatherman* and *The Resurrection of John Frum* (Theatre Projects Manitoba). Michael is the Artistic Producer of Winnipeg Jewish Theatre and a member of the Playwrights Guild of Canada.

Michael lives in Winnipeg and is married to Rebecca Brask, and has two glorious children, Zevi and Naomi.